UNLOCKING THE HIDDE

I0018043

A DEEP DIVE INTO VECTOR DATABASE

OLIVER LUCAS JR

Copyright © 2024 by Oliver Lucas Jr

All rights reserved. No part of this publication may be reproduced, distributed, or transmitted in any form or by any means, including photocopying, recording, or other electronic or mechanical methods, without the prior written permission of the publisher, except in the case of brief quotations embodied in critical reviews and certain other non commercial uses permitted by copyright law.

Preface

Unlocking the Power of Vector Databases

In an era defined by data explosion and the increasing complexity of information, the ability to efficiently search, analyze, and understand data is paramount. Vector databases, with their capacity to represent data as numerical vectors, offer a powerful tool to address these challenges.

This book is a comprehensive guide to the world of vector databases. It explores the fundamental concepts, key techniques, and practical applications of these innovative databases. From understanding the basics of vectors and embeddings to delving into advanced topics like similarity search, anomaly detection, and hybrid search, this book covers it all.

Whether you're a data scientist, machine learning engineer, or simply curious about the future of data technology, this book will equip you with the knowledge and skills to harness the power of vector databases. You'll learn how to:

Understand the Basics: Grasp the core concepts of vectors, embeddings, and similarity search.

Build Vector Databases: Learn how to design, implement, and optimize vector databases.

Leverage Advanced Techniques: Explore advanced techniques like hybrid search, anomaly detection, and clustering.

Apply Vector Databases to Real-World Problems: Discover practical applications in various domains, including search, recommendation systems, and computer vision.

As you embark on this journey, remember that vector databases are a rapidly evolving field. By staying updated with the latest trends and innovations, you can continue to push the boundaries of what's possible with data.

I hope this book serves as a valuable resource and inspires you to explore the exciting world of vector databases.

Let's dive in!

TABLE OF CONTENTS

Chapter 1

Chapter 2

Chapter 3

Chapter 4

Chapter 5

Chapter 6

Chapter 7

Chapter 8

Chapter 9

Chapter 10

Chapter 1

Introduction to Vector Databases

1.1 What is a Vector Database?

A Vector Database is a specialized database designed to store and efficiently retrieve data represented as vectors.

What are vectors? Vectors are mathematical representations of data points in a multi-dimensional space. Each dimension corresponds to a specific feature or characteristic of the data. For example, a vector representing a product might have dimensions for price, color, brand, and customer reviews.

Why use a vector database?

Similarity Search: Vector databases excel at finding items similar to a given query vector. This is particularly useful for applications like:

Semantic Search: Finding documents or information based on meaning and context, rather than exact keywords.

Recommendation Systems: Recommending products, movies, or articles based on user preferences and past behavior.

Image and Video Search: Searching for similar images or videos based on visual content.

Efficient Retrieval: Vector databases are optimized for fast search and retrieval of high-dimensional data.

Scalability: They can handle large datasets and complex queries efficiently.

How does it work?

Vectorization: Data is converted into numerical representations (vectors) using techniques like:

Word Embeddings: Mapping words to dense vectors.

Image Embeddings: Extracting visual features from images.

Text Embeddings: Representing text documents as vectors.

Indexing: Vectors are indexed in a way that allows for efficient similarity search.

Querying: When a query is made, it's converted into a vector, and the database searches for the most similar vectors.

By leveraging vector databases, organizations can unlock the power of unstructured data and build innovative applications that understand the nuances of human language and visual content.

1.2 Why Vector Databases?

Vector databases offer a powerful solution to overcome the limitations of traditional text-based search and enable a new era of intelligent applications. Here's why:

1. Semantic Search and Contextual Understanding

Beyond Keywords: Vector databases allow you to search for information based on meaning and context, rather than just exact keywords. This enables more accurate and relevant search results.

Natural Language Queries: Users can ask questions in natural language, and the database can understand the intent and provide accurate answers

2. Enhanced Recommendation Systems

Personalized Recommendations: By analyzing user behavior and preferences, vector databases can recommend products, articles, or content that aligns with individual tastes.

Collaborative Filtering: They can identify similar users and recommend items that they might like based on shared preferences.

3. Efficient Similarity Search

High-Dimensional Data: Vector databases are optimized to handle high-dimensional data, making them ideal for tasks like image and video search, where each data point is represented by a large number of features.

Fast Retrieval: They offer fast and efficient retrieval of similar items, even in large datasets.

4. Advanced Analytics and Machine Learning

Anomaly Detection: By identifying outliers in vector space,vector databases can help detect anomalies and potential security threats.

Clustering: They can group similar data points together, enabling insights and pattern discovery.

5. Powering AI and Machine Learning Applications

Model Deployment: Vector databases provide a robust platform for deploying and serving machine learning models, especially those that rely on embeddings.

Real-time Inference: They can enable real-time inference and decision-making by quickly retrieving relevant information from the database.

In summary, vector databases are revolutionizing the way we interact with data, enabling more intelligent, efficient, and personalized applications.

1.3 Key Concepts and Terminology

To fully understand vector databases, it's essential to grasp some fundamental concepts:

Core Concepts

Vector: A mathematical representation of data points in a multi-dimensional space. Each dimension corresponds to a specific feature or characteristic of the data.

Embedding: A dense vector representation of a piece of data, such as a word, document, or image. Embeddings capture semantic and syntactic information.

Similarity Search: The process of finding data points that are similar to a query vector. This is often measured using metrics like cosine similarity or Euclidean distance.

Index: A data structure that organizes vectors to facilitate efficient similarity search.

Query Vector: A vector representation of a search query.

Key Terminology

Vector Database: A specialized database designed to store and efficiently retrieve vector data.

Semantic Search: Searching for information based on meaning and context, rather than exact keywords.

Recommendation Systems: Systems that suggest relevant items to users based on their preferences and behavior.

Anomaly Detection: Identifying data points that deviate significantly from the norm.

Clustering: Grouping similar data points together.

Cosine Similarity: A measure of similarity between two non-zero vectors of an inner product space.

Euclidean Distance: The straight-line distance between two points in Euclidean space.

By understanding these concepts and terminology, you'll be well-equipped to explore the world of vector databases and their applications.

Chapter 2

Understanding Vectors and Embeddings

2.1 The Concept of Vectors

A vector is a mathematical object that possesses both magnitude (size or length) and direction. It's often visualized as an arrow, where the length represents the magnitude and the arrowhead indicates the direction.

Key characteristics of vectors:

Magnitude: The length or size of the vector.

Direction: The orientation of the vector in space.

Vector Representation

Vectors can be represented in various ways:

Geometric Representation:

As an arrow in a coordinate system.

The length of the arrow represents the magnitude, and its direction indicates the vector's orientation.

Algebraic Representation:

As an ordered list of numbers, called components.

Each component represents the vector's projection onto a specific axis in a coordinate system.

1. For example, a 2D vector can be represented as:

v = [x, y]

2.
3. where:
   ○ x is the component along the x-axis.
   ○ y is the component along the y-axis.
4. Similarly, a 3D vector can be represented as:

v = [x, y, z]

5.
6.

Vector Operations

Several operations can be performed on vectors, including:

Vector Addition: Adding two vectors component-wise.

Vector Subtraction: Subtracting one vector from another component-wise.

Scalar Multiplication: Multiplying a vector by a scalar (a number).

Dot Product: A mathematical operation that takes two equal-length sequences of numbers (usually coordinates) and returns a single number.

Cross Product: A binary operation on two vectors in three-dimensional space that results in a vector perpendicular to both.

Applications of Vectors

Vectors are fundamental to many fields, including:

Physics: Representing forces, velocities, accelerations, and fields.

Computer Graphics: Modeling 3D objects and simulating lighting and shadows.

Machine Learning: Representing data points and performing calculations like similarity and distance.

Robotics: Controlling robot movements and navigation.

Game Development: Simulating physics, character movement, and projectile trajectories.

In the context of vector databases, vectors are used to represent data points, such as text documents, images, or audio files. By converting data into numerical vectors, vector databases can efficiently store and retrieve information based on similarity rather than exact keywords.

2.2 Creating Embeddings: A Deep Dive

Embeddings are dense vector representations of data, such as words, sentences, or images. They capture the semantic and syntactic meaning of the data, allowing for powerful similarity search and machine learning applications.

How are Embeddings Created?

Embeddings are typically generated using neural network models trained on massive datasets. These models learn to map input data to dense vectors that capture the underlying relationships between data points.

Key techniques for creating embeddings:

Word Embeddings:

Word2Vec: This technique trains a neural network to predict the context of a word given its surrounding words. The learned weights of the model's hidden layer represent word embeddings.

GloVe: This method combines global word-word co-occurrence statistics with local context information to learn word embeddings.

BERT and RoBERTa: These state-of-the-art language models use a transformer architecture to capture complex linguistic relationships and generate highly accurate word embeddings.

Sentence Embeddings:

Sentence Transformers: These models extend word embedding techniques to capture the meaning of entire sentences.

BERT Sentence Embeddings: By averaging the word embeddings of words in a sentence, BERT can generate sentence embeddings.

Image Embeddings:

Convolutional Neural Networks (CNNs): CNNs are trained on large image datasets to extract visual features. The output of the final layer of a CNN can be used as an image embedding.

Vision Transformers: These models use a transformer architecture to process images in a sequence of patches, generating image embeddings that capture both local and global features.

Applications of Embeddings

Semantic Search: Finding documents or information based on meaning and context.

Recommendation Systems: Recommending products, movies, or articles based on user preferences.

Natural Language Processing: Tasks like text classification, sentiment analysis, and machine translation.

Computer Vision: Image and video search, object detection, and image generation.

By leveraging embeddings, vector databases can unlock the power of unstructured data and enable a new era of intelligent applications.

2.3 Popular Embedding Techniques

Several popular techniques are used to create embeddings, each with its own strengths and weaknesses. Here are some of the most widely used:

Word Embeddings

Word2Vec:

Trains a neural network to predict the context of a word given its surrounding words.

Captures semantic and syntactic relationships between words.

GloVe:

Combines global word-word co-occurrence statistics with local context information.

Produces embeddings that are often more accurate for tasks like word analogy and similarity.

BERT and RoBERTa:

Powerful language models that use a transformer architecture to capture complex linguistic relationships.

Generate highly accurate word embeddings that can be fine-tuned for specific tasks.

Sentence Embeddings

Sentence Transformers:

Extend word embedding techniques to capture the meaning of entire sentences.

Can be used for tasks like semantic search, text classification, and clustering.

BERT Sentence Embeddings:

Average the word embeddings of words in a sentence to create a sentence embedding.

Simple to implement but may not capture complex semantic relationships as well as specialized sentence embedding models.

Image Embeddings

Convolutional Neural Networks (CNNs):

Extract visual features from images by applying filters and pooling operations.

The output of the final layer can be used as an image embedding.

Vision Transformers:

Process images in a sequence of patches, capturing both local and global features.

Produce highly accurate image embeddings for tasks like image classification, object detection, and image generation.

By understanding these popular embedding techniques, you can choose the right approach for your specific application and effectively leverage vector databases to unlock the power of unstructured data.

Chapter 3

Core Concepts of Vector Databases

3.1 Data Storage and Indexing

Data Storage

Vector databases store data in a specialized format that enables efficient similarity search. This typically involves:

Vector Storage: The actual numerical representations of the data points, stored in a suitable format (e.g., dense or sparse vectors).

Metadata Storage: Additional information about the data, such as source, creation date, or other relevant attributes. This metadata can be used for filtering and faceting.

Indexing

Indexing is a crucial aspect of vector database performance. It involves creating data structures that allow for efficient retrieval of similar vectors. Here are some common indexing techniques:

Approximate Nearest Neighbors (ANN) Indexes:

HNSW (Hierarchical Navigable Small World): A graph-based index that efficiently finds approximate nearest neighbors in high-dimensional spaces.

Annoy (Approximate Nearest Neighbors Oh Yeah): A forest of trees that can be used to quickly find approximate nearest neighbors.

Faiss (Facebook AI Similarity Search): A library that provides efficient implementations of various ANN index algorithms.

Product Quantization (PQ):

Divides each vector into smaller subvectors (product quantizers).

Indexes each subvector separately, reducing the dimensionality of the search space.

Efficient for large-scale datasets.

Locality-Sensitive Hashing (LSH):

Maps similar vectors to the same hash buckets.

Can be used for approximate nearest neighbor search and clustering.

Choosing the Right Indexing Technique

The choice of indexing technique depends on several factors:

Dataset Size: For large datasets, techniques like PQ and HNSW can be more efficient.

Query Load: If the database is frequently queried, a fast index like HNSW or Annoy is preferred.

Accuracy Requirements: If high accuracy is critical, techniques like HNSW or Faiss can be used.

Hardware and Software Constraints: The available hardware and software infrastructure can influence the choice of index.

By understanding the principles of data storage and indexing, you can effectively leverage vector databases to build powerful applications.

3.2 Similarity Search Techniques

Similarity search is a fundamental operation in vector databases. It involves finding data points that are similar to a given query vector. Here are some common techniques:

Exact Nearest Neighbor Search

Brute Force: Directly compares the query vector to every vector in the database. While simple, it can be computationally expensive for large datasets.

Approximate Nearest Neighbor (ANN) Search

ANN search techniques aim to find approximate nearest neighbors efficiently, often sacrificing exactness for speed. Some popular ANN techniques include:

HNSW (Hierarchical Navigable Small World): Builds a hierarchical graph structure to efficiently navigate the search space.

Annoy (Approximate Nearest Neighbors Oh Yeah): Creates a forest of trees to index the data, allowing for fast approximate nearest neighbor search.

Faiss (Facebook AI Similarity Search): A library that provides efficient implementations of various ANN algorithms, including HNSW, Annoy, and others.

Locality-Sensitive Hashing (LSH)

LSH maps similar vectors to the same hash buckets, allowing for efficient similarity search. It's particularly useful for large-scale datasets.

Product Quantization (PQ)

PQ divides each vector into smaller subvectors (product quantizers). By indexing each subvector separately, PQ reduces the dimensionality of the search space, leading to faster search times.

Choosing the Right Technique

The choice of similarity search technique depends on factors such as:

Dataset Size: For large datasets, ANN techniques like HNSW and Annoy are often more efficient.

Query Load: If the database is frequently queried, fast techniques like LSH or PQ can be used.

Accuracy Requirements: If high accuracy is critical, techniques like brute force or exact nearest neighbor search can be used, but they may be computationally expensive.

Hardware and Software Constraints: The available hardware and software infrastructure can influence the choice of technique.

By understanding the different similarity search techniques, you can choose the right approach to optimize the performance of your vector database applications.

3.3 Vector Database Operations

Vector databases support a variety of operations to efficiently store, retrieve, and analyze vector data. Here are some common operations:

1. Vector Insertion

Ingesting Data: Adding new vectors to the database, typically along with associated metadata.

Batch Insertion: Inserting multiple vectors in a single operation for efficiency.

2. Vector Search

Similarity Search: Finding the most similar vectors to a given query vector.

Range Search: Retrieving vectors within a specific distance range from a query vector.

K-Nearest Neighbors (KNN): Finding the K most similar vectors to a query vector.

3. Vector Update

Modifying Existing Vectors: Updating the values of existing vectors.

Deleting Vectors: Removing vectors from the database.

4. Vector Filtering

Filtering by Metadata: Retrieving vectors based on specific metadata attributes (e.g., source, timestamp).

Combining Similarity Search and Filtering: Combining similarity search with metadata filtering for more precise results.

5. Vector Transformation

Vector Normalization: Scaling vectors to a unit length to improve similarity comparisons.

Vector Projection: Projecting vectors onto a lower-dimensional space to reduce computational cost.

6. Vector Clustering

Grouping Similar Vectors: Identifying clusters of similar vectors using techniques like K-means or DBSCAN.

Anomaly Detection: Identifying outliers or anomalies in the data.

Vector databases are designed to handle these operations efficiently, often leveraging specialized indexing techniques and hardware acceleration to achieve high performance. By mastering these operations, you can unlock the full potential of vector databases for a wide range of applications.

Chapter 4

Building a Vector Database

4.1 Choosing the Right Vector Database

Selecting the appropriate vector database for your specific needs is crucial. Here are some key factors to consider:

1. Scalability:

Data Volume: How much data do you expect to store?

Query Load: How many queries will the database need to handle per second?

Scalability Requirements: Can the database handle increasing data volumes and query loads?

2. Performance:

Query Latency: How quickly does the database need to return search results?

Indexing Efficiency: How efficiently can the database index and search large datasets?

Hardware Acceleration: Does the database support GPU acceleration for faster computations?

3. Features:

Similarity Search: Does the database support various similarity search algorithms (e.g., HNSW, Annoy, Faiss)?

Filtering and Faceting: Can you filter and facet results based on metadata?

Hybrid Search: Does the database support combining text-based and vector-based search?

Anomaly Detection and Clustering: Does the database offer built-in support for these tasks?

4. Integration:

API and SDKs: Does the database provide easy-to-use APIs and SDKs for integration with your application?

Cloud Integration: Can the database be deployed on cloud platforms like AWS, GCP, or Azure?

5. Cost:

Licensing Costs: Are there licensing fees associated with the database?

Cloud Costs: If using a cloud-based solution, consider storage and compute costs.

Popular Vector Database Options:

Pinecone: A cloud-native vector database designed for real-time search and recommendations.

Weaviate: A cloud-native vector search engine that combines semantic search with traditional search.

Milvus: An open-source vector database that supports a wide range of similarity search algorithms and features.

Faiss: An open-source library for efficient similarity search and clustering of dense vectors.

By carefully considering these factors and evaluating the available options, you can select the right vector database to power your applications.

4.2 Data Ingestion and Preparation

Data ingestion and preparation are critical steps in building a vector database. Here's a breakdown of the key steps involved:

1. Data Collection

Identify Data Sources: Determine where your data will come from (e.g., databases, files, APIs).

Data Extraction: Extract data from various sources using tools like ETL pipelines or custom scripts.

2. Data Cleaning and Preprocessing

Data Cleaning: Remove noise, inconsistencies, and errors from the data.

Data Normalization: Transform data into a consistent format (e.g., lowercase, removing stop words).

Data Tokenization: Break text data into tokens (words or subwords).

3. Feature Extraction

Text Data: Use techniques like TF-IDF, word embeddings (Word2Vec, BERT), or sentence embeddings to extract features.

Image Data: Use CNNs to extract visual features.

Audio Data: Use audio processing techniques to extract audio features.

4. Vectorization

Convert Features to Vectors: Transform extracted features into numerical representations, often using techniques like:

Dense Vectorization: Representing data as dense vectors.

Sparse Vectorization: Representing data as sparse vectors to reduce memory usage.

5. Data Loading

Batch Loading: Load large amounts of data in batches to improve performance.

Stream Loading: Continuously load data as it arrives, keeping the database up-to-date.

6. Data Validation

Verify Data Integrity: Ensure that the data is accurate and consistent.

Check Vector Quality: Validate the quality of the generated vectors.

Best Practices

Data Quality: Ensure high-quality data to improve search accuracy.

Efficient Data Loading: Use optimized techniques to minimize loading time.

Data Versioning: Implement a version control system to track changes in the data.

Data Security: Protect sensitive data with appropriate security measures.

By following these steps and best practices, you can effectively ingest and prepare data for your vector database, ensuring optimal performance and accurate search results.

4.3 Indexing and Query Optimization

Indexing and query optimization are crucial for efficient vector database operations. Here's a breakdown of these concepts:

Indexing

Indexing involves creating data structures that allow for efficient retrieval of similar vectors. Key indexing techniques include:

Approximate Nearest Neighbors (ANN) Indexes:

HNSW (Hierarchical Navigable Small World): A graph-based index that efficiently finds approximate nearest neighbors in high-dimensional spaces.

Annoy (Approximate Nearest Neighbors Oh Yeah): A forest of trees that can be used to quickly find approximate nearest neighbors.

Faiss (Facebook AI Similarity Search): A library that provides efficient implementations of various ANN index algorithms.

Product Quantization (PQ):

Divides each vector into smaller subvectors (product quantizers).

Indexes each subvector separately, reducing the dimensionality of the search space.

Efficient for large-scale datasets.

Locality-Sensitive Hashing (LSH):

Maps similar vectors to the same hash buckets.

Can be used for approximate nearest neighbor search and clustering.

Query Optimization

Query optimization techniques aim to improve the performance of vector database queries:

Query Filtering: Reduce the search space by filtering vectors based on metadata or other criteria.

Query Vector Normalization: Normalize query vectors to ensure consistent similarity comparisons.

Index Selection: Choose the appropriate index for the query based on the query type and data distribution.

Batching Queries: Combine multiple similar queries into a single batch to improve performance.

Hardware Acceleration: Leverage GPU acceleration for computationally intensive tasks like vector similarity calculations.

Best Practices

Regular Index Maintenance: Keep indexes up-to-date as data changes.

Monitor Query Performance: Track query latency and optimize accordingly.

Experiment with Different Indexes: Try different indexing techniques to find the best fit for your use case.

Consider Hardware Acceleration: Use GPUs or specialized hardware for faster computations.

Optimize Query Parameters: Fine-tune query parameters (e.g., search radius, number of results) to balance accuracy and performance.

By understanding and applying these indexing and query optimization techniques, you can significantly improve the performance of your vector database applications.

Chapter 5

Advanced Vector Database Features

5.1 Hybrid Search: Combining Text and Vector Search

Hybrid search combines the power of traditional text-based search with the semantic capabilities of vector search. This approach allows users to search for information using both keywords and natural language queries.

Key Benefits of Hybrid Search

Enhanced Search Relevance: By leveraging both keyword matching and semantic understanding, hybrid search can deliver more relevant results.

Improved User Experience: Users can search using natural language, making the search process more intuitive and efficient.

Better Handling of Complex Queries: Hybrid search can handle complex queries that involve multiple concepts and relationships.

How Hybrid Search Works

Text-Based Search: The query is tokenized, and keywords are extracted.

Vector-Based Search: The query is converted into a vector representation using techniques like sentence embeddings.

Combined Search: The results from text-based and vector-based searches are combined and ranked based on relevance.

Result Ranking: A ranking algorithm is used to determine the order of search results, considering factors like keyword match, semantic similarity, and metadata.

Implementation Strategies

Separate Indexes: Maintain separate indexes for text-based and vector-based search, and combine the results during query processing.

Hybrid Index: Create a hybrid index that combines both text and vector information, allowing for efficient search across both modalities.

Machine Learning Models: Use machine learning models to rank search results based on a combination of text-based and semantic factors.

Example Use Cases

E-commerce: Search for products using both keywords (e.g., "blue shirt") and natural language queries (e.g., "casual outfit for summer").

Enterprise Search: Find documents, emails, and other content within an organization using both keyword-based and semantic search.

Customer Support: Answer customer queries using a combination of knowledge base articles and semantic understanding.

By leveraging the strengths of both text-based and vector-based search, hybrid search can provide a more powerful and flexible search experience.

5.2 Filtering and Faceting

Filtering and faceting are powerful techniques to refine search results and provide a better user experience.

Filtering

Filtering involves narrowing down the search results based on specific criteria. In the context of vector databases, filtering can be done using both vector-based and metadata-based criteria:

Vector-Based Filtering:

Similarity Threshold: Filtering results based on a minimum similarity score to the query vector.

Distance-Based Filtering: Filtering results based on a maximum distance from the query vector.

Metadata-Based Filtering:

Attribute-Based Filtering: Filtering results based on specific attributes like product category, brand, or price range.

Range-Based Filtering: Filtering results within a specific range of numerical values (e.g., price between $100 and $200).

Faceting

Faceting involves grouping search results by specific attributes, allowing users to drill down into the data. Common facets in vector databases include:

Category Facets: Grouping results by product category, document type, or other categorical attributes.

Range Facets: Grouping results by numerical ranges (e.g., price ranges, date ranges).

Hierarchical Facets: Grouping results by hierarchical categories (e.g., country, state, city).

Example:

Consider a product search scenario. Users might want to filter products by price range (e.g., $0-$100, $100-$200, $200+) and category (e.g., electronics, clothing, books). They might also want to facet the results by brand to further refine the search.

Implementation Considerations:

Efficient Filtering: Use indexing techniques to optimize filtering performance.

Dynamic Faceting: Update facets in real-time as users interact with the search interface.

User Interface: Design a user-friendly interface to display filters and facets.

By effectively combining filtering and faceting, vector databases can provide a highly customizable and efficient search experience.

5.3 Anomaly Detection and Clustering

Vector databases can be used to perform advanced analytics tasks such as anomaly detection and clustering.

Anomaly Detection

Anomaly detection involves identifying data points that deviate significantly from the norm. In the context of vector databases, anomalies can be detected by:

Distance-Based Methods: Identifying vectors that are significantly distant from their nearest neighbors.

Density-Based Methods: Identifying vectors that lie in low-density regions of the vector space.

Statistical Methods: Using statistical techniques to identify outliers based on statistical measures like standard deviation or z-scores.

Applications of Anomaly Detection:

Fraud Detection: Identifying fraudulent transactions or behavior.

Network Security: Detecting malicious network traffic.

System Monitoring: Identifying system failures or performance issues.

Clustering

Clustering involves grouping similar data points together. In vector databases, clustering can be performed using:

K-Means Clustering: Dividing data into K clusters based on distance.

Hierarchical Clustering: Creating a hierarchy of clusters, starting from individual data points and merging them into larger clusters.

Density-Based Clustering (DBSCAN): Grouping together points that are closely packed together.

Applications of Clustering:

Customer Segmentation: Grouping customers based on similar behaviors and preferences.

Document Clustering: Grouping similar documents together for better organization and search.

Image Clustering: Grouping similar images together for image categorization and retrieval.

Vector Database Tools for Anomaly Detection and Clustering

Many vector databases offer built-in or integrated tools for anomaly detection and clustering. These tools often leverage advanced machine learning algorithms and statistical techniques.

By effectively utilizing these techniques, vector databases can provide valuable insights into data and help organizations make informed decisions.

Chapter 6

Real-World Applications of Vector Databases

6.1 Semantic Search and Question Answering

Semantic search and question answering are powerful applications of vector databases.

Semantic Search

Semantic search goes beyond keyword matching to understand the underlying meaning and context of a query. By leveraging vector embeddings, semantic search can return more relevant results, even when the query doesn't exactly match the keywords in the documents.

Key steps in semantic search:

Query Embedding: Convert the user's query into a dense vector representation.

Document Embedding: Convert documents or text passages into dense vector representations.

Similarity Search: Find the documents whose embeddings are most similar to the query embedding.

Ranking: Rank the results based on similarity scores and other factors like relevance and freshness.

Question Answering

Question answering systems aim to provide concise and informative answers to user queries. Vector databases can be used to power question answering systems by:

Document Retrieval: Retrieve relevant documents from a knowledge base using semantic search.

Answer Extraction: Extract relevant information from the retrieved documents.

Answer Generation: Generate concise and informative answers based on the extracted information.

Challenges and Considerations:

Contextual Understanding: Understanding the context of a query can be challenging, especially for complex queries.

Ambiguity Resolution: Resolving ambiguities in queries and documents is crucial for accurate results.

Fact Checking: Ensuring the accuracy of the information presented in the answers.

Ethical Considerations: Addressing biases and ensuring fairness in the results.

Vector Databases for Semantic Search and Question Answering

Vector databases provide an efficient way to store and retrieve vector embeddings, making them ideal for semantic search and question answering applications. By leveraging techniques like:

Word Embeddings: Capturing the semantic meaning of words.

Sentence Embeddings: Capturing the meaning of entire sentences.

Document Embeddings: Capturing the meaning of entire documents.

Vector databases enable more sophisticated and accurate search and question answering capabilities.

6.2 Recommendation Systems

Recommendation systems are a powerful application of vector databases, enabling personalized recommendations based on user preferences and behavior.

How Vector Databases Power Recommendation Systems:

User and Item Embeddings:

User Embeddings: Represent users as vectors in a high-dimensional space, capturing their preferences, demographics, and behavior.

Item Embeddings: Represent items (e.g., products, movies, articles) as vectors, capturing their features and attributes.

Similarity-Based Recommendations:

Collaborative Filtering: Find users with similar preferences and recommend items they've liked.

Content-Based Filtering: Recommend items similar to those a user has interacted with in the past.

Hybrid Recommendations:

Combine collaborative filtering and content-based filtering to provide more accurate and diverse recommendations.

Key Techniques:

Nearest Neighbor Search: Find items that are most similar to a user's preferred items.

Matrix Factorization: Decompose user-item interaction matrices into latent factors to discover hidden relationships.

Deep Learning Models: Use neural networks to learn complex patterns in user-item interactions.

Challenges and Considerations:

Cold Start Problem: Recommending items to new users with limited interaction history.

Sparsity: Handling sparse user-item interaction matrices.

Scalability: Recommending items to a large number of users in real-time.

Serendipity: Balancing personalized recommendations with serendipitous discoveries.

Vector Database Benefits for Recommendation Systems:

Efficient Similarity Search: Quickly find similar users and items.

Scalability: Handle large-scale recommendation systems.

Flexibility: Adapt to different recommendation strategies and algorithms.

Real-time Recommendations: Provide timely recommendations as user behavior changes.

By leveraging the power of vector databases, recommendation systems can deliver highly personalized and relevant recommendations to users, improving customer satisfaction and driving business growth.

6.3 Image and Video Search

Vector databases are revolutionizing image and video search by enabling efficient similarity search based on visual content.

Key Techniques:

Feature Extraction:

Convolutional Neural Networks (CNNs): Extract high-level features from images and videos.

Computer Vision Techniques: Use techniques like SIFT, SURF, and HOG to extract low-level features.

Vectorization:

Convert extracted features into dense vectors.

Similarity Search:

Find images or videos that are visually similar to a query image or video by comparing their vector representations.

Applications of Image and Video Search:

Image Search Engines: Search for images based on visual content, such as color, texture, or objects.

Video Search: Find videos based on visual content, such as specific scenes or actions.

Reverse Image Search: Identify the source of an image by searching for similar images online.

Product Search: Find similar products based on visual appearance.

Medical Image Analysis: Analyze medical images to detect anomalies or diagnose diseases.

Challenges and Considerations:

Feature Extraction: Extracting meaningful features from images and videos can be challenging, especially for complex scenes.

Scalability: Handling large image and video datasets efficiently.

Real-Time Search: Providing real-time search results for large-scale datasets.

Privacy and Security: Protecting sensitive visual data.

Vector Database Benefits for Image and Video Search:

Efficient Similarity Search: Quickly find visually similar images and videos.

Scalability: Handle large-scale image and video databases.

Flexibility: Adapt to different image and video search tasks.

Real-Time Search: Enable real-time search for interactive applications.

By leveraging the power of vector databases, image and video search can become more accurate, efficient, and personalized.

Chapter 7

Performance Optimization and Scalability

7.1 Indexing Strategies

Indexing is a critical aspect of vector database performance. It involves creating data structures that allow for efficient retrieval of similar vectors. Here are some common indexing strategies:

Approximate Nearest Neighbors (ANN) Indexes

ANN indexes are designed to find approximate nearest neighbors efficiently, often sacrificing exactness for speed. Some popular ANN index techniques include:

HNSW (Hierarchical Navigable Small World): Builds a hierarchical graph structure to efficiently navigate the search space.

Annoy (Approximate Nearest Neighbors Oh Yeah): Creates a forest of trees to index the data, allowing for fast approximate nearest neighbor search.

Faiss (Facebook AI Similarity Search): A library that provides efficient implementations of various ANN index algorithms.

Product Quantization (PQ)

PQ divides each vector into smaller subvectors (product quantizers). By indexing each subvector separately, PQ reduces the dimensionality of the search space, leading to faster search times.

Locality-Sensitive Hashing (LSH)

LSH maps similar vectors to the same hash buckets, allowing for efficient similarity search. It's particularly useful for large-scale datasets.

Choosing the Right Indexing Strategy

The choice of indexing strategy depends on various factors:

Dataset Size: For large datasets, techniques like PQ and HNSW can be more efficient.

Query Load: If the database is frequently queried, fast techniques like LSH or Annoy can be used.

Accuracy Requirements: If high accuracy is critical, techniques like brute force or exact nearest neighbor search can be used, but they may be computationally expensive.

Hardware and Software Constraints: The available hardware and software infrastructure can influence the choice of technique.

By carefully considering these factors and experimenting with different indexing strategies, you can optimize the performance of your vector database.

7.2 Query Optimization Techniques

Query optimization is essential for ensuring the efficient execution of queries in vector databases. Here are some key techniques:

1. Filtering

Metadata Filtering: Reduce the search space by filtering vectors based on metadata attributes (e.g., date, category, language).

Range Filtering: Filter vectors based on numerical ranges (e.g., price, age).

2. Index Selection

Choose the Right Index: Select the appropriate index for the query based on the query type and data distribution.

Combine Indexes: Use multiple indexes to optimize different query patterns.

3. Query Vector Normalization

Normalize Query Vectors: Ensure consistent similarity comparisons by normalizing query vectors.

4. Batching Queries

Combine Multiple Queries: Process multiple similar queries in a single batch to improve efficiency.

5. Hardware Acceleration

Leverage GPUs: Utilize GPU acceleration for computationally intensive tasks like vector similarity calculations.

6. Query Caching

Cache Query Results: Store frequently executed queries and their results to reduce processing time.

7. Query Rewriting

Optimize Query Syntax: Rewrite queries to improve execution efficiency.

Break Down Complex Queries: Break down complex queries into simpler subqueries.

Best Practices

Monitor Query Performance: Track query execution time and identify bottlenecks.

Profile Queries: Use profiling tools to analyze query execution plans.

Experiment with Different Techniques: Try different query optimization techniques to find the best approach.

Consider the Trade-off Between Accuracy and Performance: Balance the need for accurate results with efficient query execution.

By implementing these query optimization techniques, you can significantly improve the performance of your vector database and provide a better user experience.

7.3 Scalability and Distributed Systems

As vector databases handle increasingly large datasets and complex queries, scalability becomes a critical concern.[1]Distributed systems provide a solution to scale vector databases horizontally, distributing the workload across multiple machines.

Key Considerations for Scalability:

Data Sharding: Partitioning the data into smaller subsets and distributing them across multiple nodes.

Query Sharding: Distributing queries across multiple nodes to improve query performance.

Data Replication: Replicating data across multiple nodes to improve fault tolerance and read performance.

Load Balancing: Distributing the workload evenly across nodes to prevent bottlenecks.

Fault Tolerance: Implementing mechanisms to handle node failures and data loss.

Distributed Vector Database Architectures

Several distributed architectures can be used for vector databases:

Shared-Nothing Architecture: Each node is independent and responsible for its own data and computations. This architecture offers high scalability and fault tolerance.

Shared-Disk Architecture: Multiple nodes share a common storage system, which can improve performance but can also be a single point of failure.

Shared-Nothing with Shared-Disk: A hybrid approach that combines the benefits of both shared-nothing and shared-disk architectures.

Challenges and Considerations:

Data Consistency: Ensuring data consistency across multiple nodes, especially when updates are involved.

Network Latency: Minimizing network latency between nodes to optimize query performance.

Data Synchronization: Keeping data synchronized across multiple nodes.

Distributed Indexing: Efficiently indexing data across multiple nodes.

Distributed Query Processing: Optimizing query execution across multiple nodes.

Best Practices for Scalability:

Choose a Scalable Database: Select a vector database that is designed for scalability and supports distributed architectures.

Optimize Data Sharding: Carefully partition data to balance load and improve query performance.

Implement Efficient Data Replication: Use replication strategies to ensure data availability and fault tolerance.

Monitor System Performance: Continuously monitor the performance of the distributed system and identify bottlenecks.

Test and Benchmark: Regularly test and benchmark the system to identify performance issues and optimize configurations.

By carefully considering these factors and implementing effective strategies, you can build scalable and reliable vector database systems to handle large-scale datasets and complex queries.

Chapter 8

Security and Privacy Considerations

8.1 Data Encryption and Security Protocols

Data security is paramount when dealing with sensitive information stored in vector databases. Here are some key encryption and security protocols to consider:

Data Encryption

Encryption at Rest: Encrypt data stored on disk to protect it from unauthorized access.

Encryption in Transit: Encrypt data transmitted over networks to prevent interception.

Key Management: Implement robust key management practices to protect encryption keys.

Security Protocols

Authentication: Authenticate users to ensure only authorized individuals can access the database.

Authorization: Control access to specific resources and operations within the database.

Access Control Lists (ACLs): Define permissions for different users and groups.

Role-Based Access Control (RBAC): Assign roles to users and grant permissions based on those roles.

Network Security: Protect the network infrastructure with firewalls, intrusion detection systems, and other security measures.

Input Validation: Validate user input to prevent injection attacks.

Regular Security Audits: Conduct regular security audits to identify vulnerabilities and weaknesses.

Best Practices

Use Strong Encryption Algorithms: Employ strong encryption algorithms like AES-256.

Regularly Update Security Patches: Keep software and libraries up-to-date with the latest security patches.

Monitor for Threats: Use security monitoring tools to detect and respond to potential threats.

Train Employees: Educate employees about security best practices and potential risks.

Implement Incident Response Plans: Have a plan in place to respond to security incidents.

Consider Data Privacy Regulations: Adhere to relevant data privacy regulations like GDPR and CCPA.

By following these guidelines, you can significantly enhance the security of your vector database and protect sensitive data.

8.2 Privacy-Preserving Techniques

Privacy-preserving techniques are essential for protecting sensitive data stored in vector databases. Here are some common techniques:

1. Differential Privacy

Adding Noise: Adding random noise to data to mask individual information.

Privacy Budgets: Controlling the amount of privacy loss.

2. Homomorphic Encryption

Encrypting Data: Encrypting data before processing, allowing computations to be performed on encrypted data.

Decrypting Results: Decrypting the results to reveal the final outcome.

3. Federated Learning

Training Models Locally: Training machine learning models on local data.

Aggregating Model Updates: Aggregating model updates from multiple parties without sharing raw data.

4. Secure Multi-Party Computation (SMPC)**

Collaborative Computation: Multiple parties collaborate to compute a function over their private inputs without revealing the inputs to each other.

5. Data Minimization

Storing Only Necessary Data: Minimize the amount of sensitive data stored in the database.

Anonymizing Data: Remove personally identifiable information from the data.

Best Practices

Privacy by Design: Incorporate privacy considerations into the design and development of the vector database system.

Regular Privacy Impact Assessments: Conduct regular assessments to identify and mitigate privacy risks.

Transparency and User Consent: Be transparent about data collection and usage practices and obtain user consent.

Data Retention Policies: Implement data retention policies to limit the storage of sensitive data.

Regular Security Audits: Conduct regular security audits to identify and address vulnerabilities.

By adopting these privacy-preserving techniques, you can protect sensitive data and build trust with users.

8.3 Regulatory Compliance

When working with vector databases, it's crucial to comply with relevant data protection and privacy regulations. Here are some key regulations to consider:

General Data Protection Regulation (GDPR)

The GDPR imposes strict requirements on how personal data is collected, processed, and stored. Key considerations for vector databases include:

Data Minimization: Only collect and store the necessary data.

Purpose Limitation: Clearly define the purpose for collecting and processing data.

Data Subject Rights: Respect individuals' rights to access, rectify, erase, and restrict processing of their data.

Data Security: Implement appropriate technical and organizational measures to protect personal data.

International Data Transfers: Ensure compliance with data transfer rules when transferring data to other countries.

California Consumer Privacy Act (CCPA)

The CCPA grants California residents specific rights regarding their personal information. Key considerations for vector databases include:

Data Collection and Sale Disclosures: Disclose the categories of personal information collected and whether it is sold or shared.

Consumer Rights: Provide consumers with the right to know, access, delete, and opt-out of the sale of their personal information.

Data Security: Implement reasonable security measures to protect personal information.

Other Regulations

Depending on the specific industry and jurisdiction, other regulations may apply, such as:

HIPAA (Health Insurance Portability and Accountability Act): For healthcare data.

PCI DSS (Payment Card Industry Data Security Standard): For[1] payment card data.

FERPA (Family Educational Rights and Privacy Act): For student education records.

Best Practices for Regulatory Compliance

Data Mapping: Map personal data to understand its flow and storage.

Data Inventory: Create an inventory of personal data assets.

Data Protection Impact Assessments (DPIAs): Conduct DPIAs to assess the privacy risks of data processing activities.

Regular Security Audits: Conduct regular security audits to identify and address vulnerabilities.

Employee Training: Train employees on data protection and privacy regulations.

Incident Response Plan: Have a plan in place to respond to data breaches.

By understanding and complying with relevant regulations, you can protect your organization and users from legal and reputational risks.

Chapter 9

The Future of Vector Databases

9.1 Emerging Trends and Innovations

The field of vector databases is rapidly evolving, with several exciting trends and innovations on the horizon:

1. Advanced Embeddings

Multimodal Embeddings: Combining information from multiple modalities (text, image, audio) into a single embedding.

Contextual Embeddings: Capturing context-specific information to improve search accuracy.

Personalized Embeddings: Tailoring embeddings to individual users' preferences and behavior.

2. Hybrid Search

Combining Text and Vector Search: Seamlessly integrating text-based and vector-based search to provide more comprehensive results.

Knowledge Graph Integration: Leveraging knowledge graphs to enhance semantic understanding and improve search accuracy.

3. Real-Time Analytics

Streaming Data: Processing and analyzing data in real-time as it is generated.

Real-Time Recommendations: Delivering personalized recommendations in real-time.

Real-Time Anomaly Detection: Identifying anomalies as they occur.

4. Privacy-Preserving Techniques

Federated Learning: Training models collaboratively without sharing raw data.

Homomorphic Encryption: Performing computations on encrypted data.

Differential Privacy: Adding noise to data to protect privacy.

5. Quantum Computing

Quantum Algorithms for Similarity Search: Developing quantum algorithms to accelerate similarity search.

Quantum Machine Learning: Leveraging quantum computing for advanced machine learning models.

6. AI-Driven Optimization

AutoML for Vector Databases: Automating the process of selecting the best algorithms and hyperparameters.

AI-Powered Query Optimization: Optimizing queries based on real-time data and system load.

By staying informed about these emerging trends and innovations, you can leverage the full potential of vector databases to build cutting-edge applications.

9.2 Potential Applications and Use Cases

Vector databases have a wide range of applications across various industries. Here are some potential applications and use cases:

1. Search and Recommendation

Semantic Search: Finding relevant information based on meaning and context.

Product Recommendation: Recommending products to customers based on their preferences and purchase history.

Content Recommendation: Recommending articles, videos, or music based on user interests.

2. Natural Language Processing

Question Answering: Answering complex questions by understanding the intent and context.

Text Summarization: Summarizing long documents or articles.

Sentiment Analysis: Analyzing the sentiment of text data.

3. Computer Vision

Image Search: Finding similar images based on visual content.

Object Detection: Identifying objects in images and videos.

Image Classification: Categorizing images based on their content.

4. Biomedicine

Drug Discovery: Identifying potential drug candidates.

Medical Image Analysis: Analyzing medical images to detect diseases.

Genomic Analysis: Analyzing genetic data to identify disease-related genes.

5. Financial Services

Fraud Detection: Identifying fraudulent transactions.

Risk Assessment: Assessing credit risk and investment risk.

Algorithmic Trading: Developing trading strategies based on market data analysis.

6. Cybersecurity

Threat Detection: Identifying malicious activities and cyberattacks.

Network Security: Monitoring network traffic for anomalies.

User Behavior Analysis: Detecting unusual user behavior.

7. Customer Service

Chatbots: Creating intelligent chatbots that can understand and respond to customer queries.

Customer Support: Providing personalized customer support.

By leveraging the power of vector databases, organizations can unlock new insights, improve decision-making, and create innovative applications.

9.3 Challenges and Opportunities

While vector databases offer significant potential, they also present challenges and opportunities:

Challenges

Data Quality: The quality of the input data directly impacts the quality of the embeddings and search results.

Computational Cost: Training and deploying large-scale vector databases can be computationally expensive.

Data Privacy: Protecting sensitive data while leveraging its power for analysis.

Model Bias: Addressing biases in the training data and models to ensure fairness and equity.

Interpretability: Understanding the reasons behind the decisions made by vector database models.

Opportunities

Innovation: Driving innovation in various industries by enabling new applications and use cases.

Improved Search: Enhancing search capabilities beyond keyword-based search to semantic search.

Personalized Experiences: Delivering highly personalized experiences to users.

Efficient Data Analysis: Accelerating data analysis and insights.

Automation: Automating tasks and processes through AI-powered solutions.

To overcome these challenges and seize the opportunities, it's essential to:

Invest in Data Quality: Ensure high-quality data to improve model performance.

Optimize Model Training and Inference: Use efficient techniques to reduce computational costs.

Prioritize Data Privacy: Implement strong security measures and privacy-preserving techniques.

Continuously Monitor and Improve Models: Regularly evaluate and refine models to maintain performance.

Collaborate with Experts: Work with domain experts and data scientists to address complex challenges.

Stay Updated with the Latest Trends: Keep up with the latest advancements in vector database technology.

By addressing these challenges and leveraging the opportunities, vector databases can revolutionize the way we interact with data and drive innovation across various industries.

Chapter 10

Conclusion

10.1 Recap of Key Concepts

Vector Databases are specialized databases designed to store and efficiently retrieve data represented as vectors. Key concepts include:

Vectors: Mathematical representations of data points in a multi-dimensional space.

Embeddings: Dense vector representations of data, capturing semantic and syntactic meaning.

Similarity Search: Finding data points that are similar to a query vector.

Indexing: Organizing vectors to facilitate efficient similarity search.

Hybrid Search: Combining text-based and vector-based search for enhanced results.

Anomaly Detection: Identifying data points that deviate significantly from the norm.

Clustering: Grouping similar data points together.

Key Techniques and Applications:

Word Embeddings: Representing words as vectors.

Sentence Embeddings: Representing sentences as vectors.

Image and Video Embeddings: Representing visual content as vectors.

Semantic Search: Finding information based on meaning and context.

Recommendation Systems: Recommending products or content based on user preferences.

Image and Video Search: Searching for images and videos based on visual content.

Anomaly Detection: Identifying outliers in data.

Clustering: Grouping similar data points together.

By understanding these concepts and techniques, you can effectively utilize vector databases to build powerful and innovative applications.

10.2 Best Practices and Tips

To effectively leverage vector databases, consider these best practices and tips:

Data Preparation:

Clean and Preprocess Data: Ensure data quality by removing noise, inconsistencies, and irrelevant information.

Choose Appropriate Embedding Techniques: Select embedding techniques that align with the specific task and data characteristics.

Optimize Vectorization: Efficiently convert data into vector representations to minimize memory usage and improve performance.

Indexing and Query Optimization:

Experiment with Different Indexes: Test various indexing techniques to find the optimal solution for your specific use case.

Optimize Query Parameters: Fine-tune query parameters (e.g., search radius, number of results) to balance accuracy and performance.

Leverage Hardware Acceleration: Utilize GPUs or specialized hardware to accelerate computationally intensive tasks.

Monitor Query Performance: Track query latency and optimize queries as needed.

Model Selection and Training:

Choose the Right Model: Select models that are suitable for the specific task and data characteristics.

Fine-Tune Models: Fine-tune pre-trained models on specific datasets to improve performance.

Regularly Retrain Models: Retrain models periodically to adapt to changes in data and user behavior.

Deployment and Monitoring:

Choose a Scalable Infrastructure: Select a scalable infrastructure to handle increasing workloads.

Monitor System Performance: Monitor system metrics, such as CPU usage, memory usage, and disk I/O.

Implement Robust Security Measures: Protect sensitive data and infrastructure from unauthorized access.

Continuously Evaluate and Improve: Regularly evaluate the performance of the vector database and make necessary adjustments.

By following these best practices and tips, you can effectively leverage vector databases to build powerful and scalable applications.

10.3 The Future of Vector Databases

The future of vector databases is bright, with numerous exciting possibilities on the horizon. Here are some key trends and predictions:

1. Advanced Embeddings

Multimodal Embeddings: Combining information from multiple modalities (text, image, audio) into a single embedding for more comprehensive search and analysis.

Contextual Embeddings: Capturing context-specific information to improve search accuracy and relevance.

Personalized Embeddings: Tailoring embeddings to individual users' preferences and behavior.

2. Hybrid Search

Seamless Integration: Further integrating text-based and vector-based search to provide a more comprehensive and intuitive search experience.

Knowledge Graph Integration: Leveraging knowledge graphs to enhance semantic understanding and improve search results.

3. Real-Time Analytics

Streaming Data: Processing and analyzing data in real-time as it is generated.

Real-Time Recommendations: Delivering personalized recommendations in real-time.

Real-Time Anomaly Detection: Identifying anomalies as they occur.

4. Privacy-Preserving Techniques

Federated Learning: Training models collaboratively without sharing raw data.

Homomorphic Encryption: Performing computations on encrypted data.

Differential Privacy: Adding noise to data to protect privacy.

5. Quantum Computing

Quantum Algorithms for Similarity Search: Developing quantum algorithms to accelerate similarity search.

Quantum Machine Learning: Leveraging quantum computing for advanced machine learning models.

6. AI-Driven Optimization

AutoML for Vector Databases: Automating the process of selecting the best algorithms and hyperparameters.

AI-Powered Query Optimization: Optimizing queries based on real-time data and system load.

By staying informed about these trends and actively exploring new possibilities, you can position yourself to harness the full potential of vector databases and drive innovation in your field.

UNLOCKING THE HIDDEN PATTERNS

HIDDEN PATTERNS

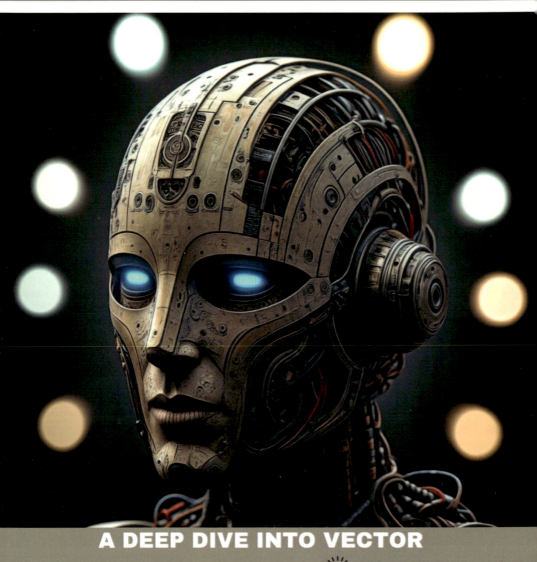

A DEEP DIVE INTO VECTOR DATABASE

OLIVER LUCAS JR